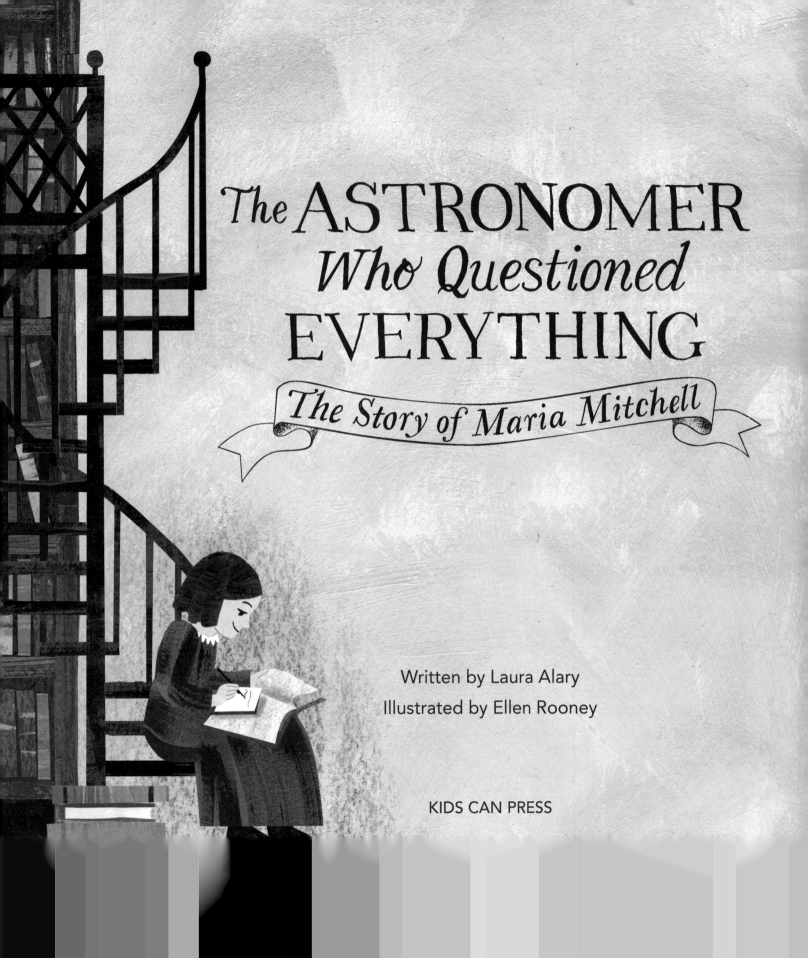

The ASTRONOMER Who Questioned EVERYTHING

The Story of Maria Mitchell

Written by Laura Alary

Illustrated by Ellen Rooney

KIDS CAN PRESS

Maria was a collector.

Stones. Shells. Feathers.

Words. Ideas.

She was always looking. Whatever sparked her
imagination, Maria tucked into her pocket or
jotted down in her notebook.

As she grew up, Maria never stopped looking. She longed to see beyond her little island of Nantucket. But how? Should she follow her brother and sail away on a whaling ship?

At sea, there are no roads, no signs, no one to show you the way. Maria knew that sailors looked to the stars for guidance. If you knew how to read them, the stars could tell you where you were, and where you needed to go.

Maria decided she would rather look for stars than whales.

Her father, an astronomer and mathematician, showed her how. On clear evenings, they climbed up to the roof, set up a telescope and spent hours scanning the sky. What they found filled Maria with wonder.

She learned to use a sextant to measure the height of stars, a metronome to track their slow creep across the dome of night, and a chronometer that measured time at sea so sailors could figure out how far east or west they had sailed.

Everything she saw and learned and wondered about, Maria collected in her notebook.

One day, a sea captain came to the door carrying a broken chronometer. He needed Maria's father to fix it before he could set sail. Without it, his crew would be lost.

Maria told him her father was away, but she could help him.

The captain wasn't so sure. What could a girl possibly know of mathematics and machines? But what choice did he have? Maria set to work, her mind whirling with numbers, calculations and measurements as tiny and precise as the springs and gears of the chronometer.

She did not make a single mistake.

When her father heard the
story, he was so proud he
gave Maria a gift: a room of
her own. It was only a closet
under the stairs, but it was
hers. A place to write, to
dream, to think in peace.

DO NOT
KNOCK.
MISS
MITCHELL
IS BUSY.

Her brother returned from sea, full of life and stories. Maria, whose days were filled with housework and caring for her younger brothers and sisters, wondered if she would ever come home from away, overflowing with tales to tell.

Maybe, her brother teased, she would prefer to stay at home, raise a houseful of children and teach them all to embroider cushions?

Maria, who hated fine needlework, swatted him with her embroidery hoop. All those tiny stitches! What was the good of them? They chained her mind to a needle.

When she walked on the shore or sat on the roof, Maria looked outside herself. But once a week, she went to the Quaker Meeting House where she practiced looking inside, too. It was quiet there. No music. No preacher. No candles. No colors. Just silence.

When she sat still, her swirling thoughts settled like tea leaves at the bottom of a cup. Then she could see clearly. She knew herself. She was a dreamer. A wonderer. A collector. She had to keep looking.

But she also had to earn a living.

How old?   celestial   how far ???   universe orbit

Maria's Journal

Maria started her own school.
But it wasn't just any school.

She led her students outdoors
so they could look at the world
for themselves.

They waded through
bogs, climbed cliffs and
peered into tidal pools.

Then Maria became a librarian. She devoted herself to reading, collecting new words and feeding her mind with ideas as sweet and juicy as oranges.

Books carried her to new places. But Maria wanted more.
So she set her sights higher.

The King of Denmark had offered a prize to the first
person to find a new comet. All over the world, in the
greatest observatories, astronomers were watching.

Night after night, Maria watched, too. She climbed up to her roof, focused her telescope and scanned the vast night sky. She was determined to find it — a distant chunk of ice and dust hurtling around the sun.

Nothing could stop Maria from looking. Not even a broken wire in the lens of her telescope. For three weeks, she struggled to repair it.

She tried using her own hair, but it was too coarse.

In the end, she unwound a silkworm cocoon and fixed the delicate threads in place with steady fingers ... and a chuckle.

All that fine needlework had been good for something after all!

And one October night, Maria found it. Her comet. A milky crescent in her telescope lens, no bigger than the tip of her fingernail. Maria Mitchell, with her small telescope on the tiny island of Nantucket, was the first person on Earth ever to see it.

Doors that had been shut tight suddenly opened. Maria strode
through them. She sailed to Europe, visited observatories, met
with astronomers and mathematicians, joined scientific societies,
listened to lectures and began to give her own.

Then came a letter from a new college for women in New York, inviting Maria to be a professor of astronomy. At last, she knew what to do with all the ideas and questions she had collected over the years.

delighted to to welcome observatory

Dear Miss Mitchell, We would you to give a lecture

VASSAR COLLEGE
UNITED STAT

nsider this offer
essor of Astronomy
Vassar coll

But the road was not without its bumps. It seemed everyone had an opinion …

Women students MUST NOT go out after dark

Maria thought this was ABSURD! How could her students watch stars by daylight?

If women spent all their time READING BOOKS, there would be no one to DO THE COOKING.

Maria thought this was RIDICULOUS! Why starve women's minds to feed men's bodies?

Too much
study is
NOT GOOD
for young
women

Maria thought this was PREPOSTEROUS!
How many women die from too much
learning? Far more likely, she thought, for
them to wither away, bored to death from
doing needlework!

For the rest of her life, Maria was a teacher. But not just any teacher. She took her students outside so they could search the night sky for themselves. She told them stories about great scientists and mathematicians, but also about faraway places and times long ago. She wanted her students to see how people have always been looking to understand the world around them.

Above all, she taught them to question everything and everyone — especially those who said women belonged at home with their sewing needles!

Now and then, Maria came home to Nantucket,
overflowing with tales to tell. She roamed the shore,
often with her nieces and nephews.

They collected things.

Stones. Shells. Feathers.

And they asked questions. So many questions!

Questions that carried them far beyond the little island of Nantucket, into the wide world and the universe beyond. Maria had taught them well. They would always keep looking.

Author's Note

Decisions, Decisions ...

None of us come into the world knowing who we are and what we want to do with our lives. We have to figure it out as we go — and that is a hard task. There can be too many choices. Or too few. You can set out boldly and get lost. Or be too afraid to take the first step. You can get stuck comparing yourself to people who seem to have more — more talent or more opportunities.

Or you can be like Maria Mitchell.

"Mingle the starlight with your eyes and you won't be fretted by trifles."

A Woman of Firsts

In 1818, American women were not allowed to vote, go to university or enter professions that required higher education. So you might think that a girl born in 1818 on a tiny island in the Atlantic to a family of ten children would have few chances to do much with her life. But no matter how unlikely it seemed, Maria (pronounced Ma-RYE-ah) would become the first professional female astronomer in the United States, the first woman member of the American Academy of Arts and Sciences, the first woman hired by the U.S. government for scientific work and one of the first female professors at Vassar, the pioneering American women's college.

PROF. M. MITCHELL

Growing Up

How did Maria do it? Part of the answer lies in where she came from — she was strongly influenced by both her family and the place where she grew up.

Maria's family were Quakers, a religious group that believes in the equality of all people. In the quiet simplicity of weekly Quaker meetings, Maria learned to listen to her own inner voice rather than looking to an authority figure to tell her what to think.

Quakers also believe in educating both girls and boys. Maria's mother had been a librarian. She shared with Maria her love of words, stories and books of all kinds. Maria's father was a schoolteacher who taught himself advanced mathematics and astronomy so he could earn extra money calculating longitude and latitude for the many whaling ships that sailed from Nantucket. He passed this skill on to his daughter, teaching her everything he knew about the science of navigation. In a seafaring community, being good at math was a valuable and practical skill.

And with so many men away at sea, it was the women of Nantucket who ran many of the inns, shops and local businesses. Maria grew up surrounded by independent women.

The Three P's:
Patience, Practice, Persistence

But there was more to Maria than her environment. She once said: "I was born of only ordinary capacity, but of extraordinary persistency." We see this persistence in her commitment to learning mathematics, in her meticulous repairs to her instruments, in the long nights she spent alone on the roof with her telescope. And we see it in her determination to read *every single book* in the Nantucket library — by the time she finished, she had given herself the equivalent of a university education and had filled many pages with her own notes and opinions. No matter how famous the authors were, Maria felt free to question and disagree.

We see Maria's persistence in how, as a professor at Vassar College, she sidestepped what she saw as pointless rules that held women back from learning, and worked diligently to create new opportunities for her female students.

The Benefits of Boredom

When she was a young woman, Maria was bored silly by the needlework she was expected to do. She thought it kept the minds of women and girls chained to meaningless activity so their thoughts were never free. But over the years, she came to see that even needlework had something to teach her: patience, precision, attention to detail, the ability to discern colors, a delicate touch and, most of all, the ability to tolerate a dull routine and keep going!

Maria understood that there is more to success than natural ability. In order to become good at something, you have to practice. And practice isn't always fun.

Question Everything!

As a teacher, Maria had high standards for her students. She expected them to work hard, to be disciplined, to observe carefully, to wonder — and to use their own minds. Maria did *not* expect her students to simply accept everything they were told because it came from a trusted source. She told her students to question everything — even what *she* taught them!

"To know what one ought to do is certainly the hardest thing in life."

Free to Choose

Although Maria was passionate about astronomy and fought hard for the advancement of women in science, what mattered most to her was freedom of *choice* — that all children should be free to learn about and pursue the things they truly love. In this, she was ahead of her time.

Not only did Maria believe women could be good scientists, she also thought that men could be good dressmakers and cooks, if that was where their interests lay. Let it be a matter of free choice!

How Do YOU Choose?

Maria knew that no one is able to choose without knowing what the choices are. She insisted that *all* children deserve the chance to learn and figure out for themselves what they want to do and be.

If you ever feel like you have no idea where you want your life to go, or whether you can get there, ask yourself, "What would Maria do?" Then …

O Grab a notebook.

O Collect things you love.

O Try one path.

O Then another.

O Sit still sometimes.

O Listen to your inner voice.

O Remember to practice.

O Let yourself be bored.

O Ask questions.

O And keep looking!

Observations

y for 11 hrs.

$(\alpha - \alpha') = -0° 30' 36''$

9 2620142
5. 9488436

Resources

Anderson, Dale. *Maria Mitchell*. Women in Science Library. Philadelphia: Chelsea House, 2003.

Atkins, Jeannine. *Finding Wonders: Three Girls Who Changed Science*. New York: Atheneum, 2016.

Bergland, Renée. *Maria Mitchell and the Sexing of Science: An Astronomer among the American Romantics*. Boston: Beacon Press, 2008.

Gormley, Beatrice. *Maria Mitchell: The Soul of an Astronomer*. Grand Rapids: Eerdmans, 1995.

Maria Mitchell Association – www.mariamitchell.org

Mitchell, Maria. *Maria Mitchell: Life, Letters, and Journals*. Online through Project Gutenberg.

Popova, Maria. *Figuring*. New York: Vintage Books, 2019.

Wright, Helen. *Sweeper in the Sky: The Life of Maria Mitchell*. New York: MacMillan, 1949.

For all the girls trying to find their way, and for the teachers who encourage them to keep looking — especially Willow and Jason — L.A.

For Mary, Maura, Kathleen, Paul and Terrence — E.R.

Text © 2022 Laura Alary
Illustrations © 2022 Ellen Rooney

Published in Canada and the U.S. by Kids Can Press Ltd.
25 Dockside Drive, Toronto, ON M5A 0B5

Kids Can Press is a Corus Entertainment Inc. company
www.kidscanpress.com

The artwork in this book was rendered in collage.
The text is set in Avenir.

Edited by Jennifer Stokes and Olga Kidisevic
Designed by Barb Kelly

Printed and bound in Buji, Shenzhen, China,
in 10/2021 by WKT Company

CM 22 0 9 8 7 6 5 4 3 2 1

Library and Archives Canada Cataloguing in Publication

Title: The astronomer who questioned everything : the story of Maria Mitchell / Laura Alary ; Ellen Rooney.
Names: Alary, Laura, author. | Rooney, Ellen, illustrator.
Identifiers: Canadiana 20210191902 | ISBN 9781525303487 (hardcover)
Subjects: LCSH: Mitchell, Maria, 1818-1889 — Juvenile literature. | LCSH: Astronomers — United States — Biography — Juvenile literature. | LCSH: Women astronomers — United States — Biography — Juvenile literature. | LCGFT: Biographies. Classification: LCC QB36.M58 A43 2022 | DDC j520.92 — dc23

Kids Can Press gratefully acknowledges that the land on which our office is located is the traditional territory of many nations, including the Mississaugas of the Credit, the Anishnabeg, the Chippewa, the Haudenosaunee and the Wendat peoples, and is now home to many diverse First Nations, Inuit and Métis peoples.

We thank the Government of Ontario, through Ontario Creates; the Ontario Arts Council; the Canada Council for the Arts; and the Government of Canada for supporting our publishing activity.